EARTH*ROCKS!*

EARTHQUAKES

BY SARA GILBERT

CREATIVE EDUCATION • CREATIVE PAPERBACKS

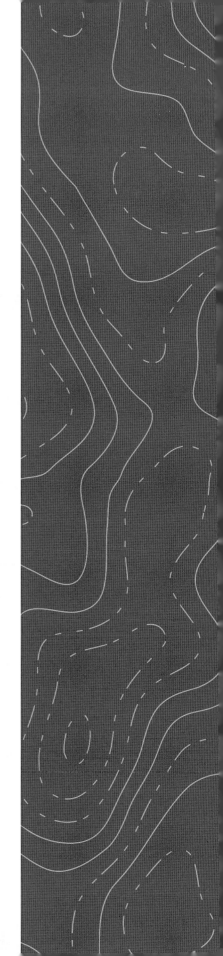

Published by Creative Education and Creative Paperbacks
P.O. Box 227, Mankato, Minnesota 56002
Creative Education and Creative Paperbacks are
imprints of The Creative Company
www.thecreativecompany.us

Design and production by Chelsey Luther
Art direction by Rita Marshall
Printed in the United States of America

Photographs by Alamy (Richard Cummins, Alexander Frolov),
Dreamstime (TMarchev), Getty Images (Lloyd Cluff/Corbis, De
Agostini/Publiaer Foto, Dorling Kindersley, Library of Congress/Corbis/
VCG, David Weintraub), iStockphoto (fabiofoto), National Geographic
Creative (JAMES P. BLAIR, GEORGE STEINMETZ), Shutterstock (Filip
Fuxa), Spoon Graphics (Chris Spooner)

Library of Congress Cataloging-in-Publication Data
Names: Gilbert, Sara.
Title: Earthquakes / Sara Gilbert.
Series: Earth Rocks!
Includes bibliographical references and index.
Summary: An elementary exploration of earthquakes, focusing on the
geological evidence that helps explain how and where they form and
spotlighting famous examples, such as the 2004 Indian Ocean quake.
Identifiers: ISBN 978-1-60818-892-5 (hardcover) / ISBN 978-1-62832-
508-9 (pbk) / ISBN 978-1-56660-944-9 (eBook)

This title has been submitted for CIP processing under
LCCN 2017937618.

CCSS: RI.1.1, 2, 4, 5, 6, 7; RI.2.2, 5, 6, 7, 10; RI.3.1, 5, 7, 8; RF.1.1, 3, 4; RF.2.3, 4

First Edition HC 9 8 7 6 5 4 3 2 1
First Edition PBK 9 8 7 6 5 4 3 2 1

*Pictured on cover: **Sicilian town (top); Icelandic fissure (bottom)***

TABLE OF CONTENTS

TAKE COVER!

Plates are rattling in the cupboard. Books are falling off the shelves. The ground is shaking. You are in the middle of an earthquake! Get under a sturdy table and hold on tight!

SAN ANDREAS FAULT, CALIFORNIA

ON THE MOVE

Huge slabs of rock cover Earth's crust like puzzle pieces. These rocks are called tectonic plates. They form faults where they meet.

The pieces are always moving.

They are trying to find a

better fit.

SHAKING UP

Earthquakes happen when two plates suddenly slide past each other. They release energy that makes the surface shake. Sometimes the ground splits apart, too.

Earthquakes start deep inside the earth. The energy moves up, layer by layer. It makes **seismic waves**.

SEISMIC WAVES

EPICENTER ⟶

BIG AND SMALL

Some earthquakes are so small that no one feels them. Others topple buildings and destroy towns. Earthquakes can make rocks and mud slide down hills. They can cause tsunamis. They can also spark volcanoes.

FINDING FAULTS

Places on active fault lines have more earthquakes. Japan, China, and Indonesia have had many quakes. California is on the San Andreas Fault. There are earthquakes there, too.

SAN ANDREAS FAULT, CALIFORNIA

SAN FRANCISCO, 1906

EARTHQUAKE EXAMPLES

On December 26, 2004, an earthquake in the Indian Ocean caused at least five tsunamis. More than 200,000 people died. In 1906, an earthquake struck San Francisco, California. People could see the land split apart.

Be careful around earthquake damage! It can be unstable. Sometimes, more earthquakes can hit, too.

ACTIVITY: MAKE A QUAKE DETECTOR

Paper

Empty shoebox

Scissors

Can of soup

Tape

Felt-tip marker that has a cap with a clip

String

1. Place a piece of paper on a table or desk.

2. Take off the shoebox lid and cut a one-inch (2.5 cm) slit in the middle of it, about an inch (2.5 cm) from the end.

3. Stand the box upright. Place the soup can inside the box to weigh it down.

4. Place the lid on top of the box to form an upside-down *L*, and tape it on.

5. Take the cap off the marker and put it on the other end of the marker. Tie the string to the clip on the cap. Then thread the other end of the string through the slit in the lid. Adjust the string so that the tip of the marker just hits the paper.

6. Slowly pull the paper under the marker. Watch what happens to the line when a friend bumps into the table or stomps her feet. This is roughly how scientists measure the movement of the earth!

GLOSSARY

crust: the outermost layer of the earth

faults: the places where sections of Earth's crust meet and move next to each other

seismic waves: waves of energy that travel through the layers of the earth

tsunamis: large waves caused by undersea earthquakes

READ MORE

Simon, Seymour. *Earthquakes*. New York: HarperCollins, 2006.

Winchester, Simon. *When the Earth Shakes*. New York: Viking, 2015.

WEBSITES

National Geographic Kids: Earthquake
http://kids.nationalgeographic.com/explore/science /earthquake/#earthquake-houses.jpg
Learn more about what happens during an earthquake.

U.S. Geological Survey: Earthquakes for Kids
http://earthquake.usgs.gov/learn/kids/
Learn earthquake facts and find out more about what scientists know about earthquakes.

Note: Every effort has been made to ensure that any websites listed above were active at the time of publication and suitable for children. However, because of the nature of the Internet, it is impossible to guarantee that these sites will remain active indefinitely or that their contents will not be altered.

INDEX